THE BONSAI YEAR BOOK

Stone Lantern Publishing Co.

First published in the United States in 1994 by
Stone Lantern Publishing Co.
P.O. Box 816
Sudbury, MA 01776

First published in Great Britain in 1994 by
Greenwood Gallery
Ollerton Road
Arnold
Nottingham NG5 8PR

ISBN No 0-9634423-1-7

THE BONSAI YEAR BOOK
was produced by Greenwood Gallery for
Stone Lantern Publishing

Concept/design/layout - **Paul Goff**
Introduction and editing - **Harry Tomlinson**
Typesetting/artwork by **Howard Fillingham**
Photography by **Paul Goff**

Printed and bound in Hong Kong by
Regent Publishing Services Limited

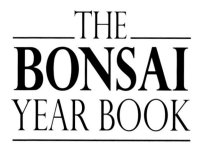

THE
BONSAI
YEAR BOOK

*The bonsai growers companion
to seasonal care & maintenance*

PAUL GOFF
in association with
HARRY TOMLINSON

Stone Lantern Publishing Co.

CONTENTS

I am happy to be writing this introduction to Paul Goff's excellent 'Bonsai Year Book', it should prove informative and useful for beginners and experienced bonsai enthusiasts alike.

I have known Paul for many years, both as a friend, colleague and fellow bonsai enthusiast, he was responsible for the superb photography in my book *"The Complete Book of Bonsai"* and has been the official photographer at many National and International Bonsai Conventions and Exhibitions.

In my experience, the photography of bonsai is far from easy and I have seen less than adequate photographs of bonsai produced by professional photographers who are very successful in other fields.

Below: Paul and Harry hard at work taking shots for the 'Bonsai Year Book'. Harry is seen offering Paul a haircut in return for the address of his tailor.

Paul's advantage is that he looks through the viewfinder not just with a photographer's eye but also with a bonsai designer's eye.

When Paul Goff approached me with his idea for me to participate with him to produce and publish his Bonsai Year Book, I thought back to the time when I initially became interested in bonsai.

My first objective was to find out more about these fascinating living works of art and how to create them myself. I soon realised that this in itself was not enough, I had to learn the practicalities of how to keep them alive and growing healthily.

Eventually came the dreadful questions that plague everyone at that stage, "When ?", "When can I re-pot safely ?", "When can I leaf cut my maple ?", "When ? When ? When ?".

Pretty soon after this stage follows the times of self doubt, "When did I last re-pot this tree ?".

"Did I feed this tree last week or last month ?".

"Should I be pinching out the pine candles now or later ?".

This book seeks to answer these first questions and others (but not, as you can see from the photograph of Paul and myself, where to get your hair cut). The book also helps to serve as an *aide memoire* as to techniques and as a notebook to record dates of re-potting, pruning and feeding etc..

I am sure that this book fills a long needed gap, giving practical seasonal guidance to instil a confident approach to year round planning and care for your bonsai.

I wish you luck and hope that all your bonsai are truly grateful.

Harry Tomlinson

Harry Tomlinson

Greenwood Gardens
Nottingham
England

The joy of watching bonsai encounter seasonal changes and the trees' responses to those changes is without doubt one of the greatest pleasures to be had by lovers of plants and horticulture. Just like their natural counterparts growing freely in the wild, bonsai will, if given appropriate care and attention, provide fabulous displays of seasonal colour, flushes of new spring growth, beautiful autumn tints and delicate details of winter silhouettes, that continue to fascinate all those who grow them.

Below: Bonsai are ideally displayed above the ground on staging and pedestals.

Seasonal care and maintenance will encourage bonsai to produce inherent natural beauty, and certain styling techniques will assist the tree in developing into an exciting living work of art.

To stimulate the tree's ability to produce such stunning displays, we need to tune in to the plant's individual requirements; will it need protection from extremes of temperature - mid summer sun and winter frosts? How much water should the trees receive? When should bonsai be fed? Are the trees likely to become pot bound and when is the correct time to repot?

In terms of horticulture, bonsai are relatively easy to keep alive. Just a little more attention will enable these trees to produce pleasing seasonal displays. Further care and some dedication to the the plant's requirements, together with styling techniques, can in time, produce a bonsai of merit, giving pleasure to all who come into its presence.

Below: The summer brilliance of Japanese maple (Acer palmatum).

Above right: Autumn provides some glowing colours as displayed on this purple beech (Fagus sylvatica purpurea).

The Bonsai Year Book has been designed as a workbook, so do not be afraid to take it outside and use it amongst your trees. It will be a helpful companion while attending to the needs of your bonsai.

Right: Juniper (Juniperus chinensis Blaauws variety) during routine thinning out.

Pages have been provided for your own notes and records which might include; feeding types and schedules; when repotted; soil types; insecticide and fungicide applications; leaf removal and countless other notes that you may need to refer to when monitoring the outcome of your tasks. The contents of this book are not intended to provide step by step guidance in producing bonsai, but to ensure that existing outdoor varieties are maintained in prime condition so they may delight and surprise us with unfolding beauty in a way that only nature can.

Below: Styling inspiration can be gained by observing trees in the wild like this common juniper, and interpretation in a bonsai juniper (Juniperus silver spreader).

Being derived from the direct effects of nature and the ravages of time, the art of bonsai has become the result of man's inspiration and need to re-create living works of art in the form of artificially dwarfed and potted trees. It is therefore quite natural that as bonsai growers, we should look back to nature for guidance when styling trees. The quiet dormant months of the bonsai calendar provide the opportunity for in depth study and observation of naturally occurring specimens for us to draw comparisons with our own creations.

To aid us in the process of styling trees, specific tools and cutters are produced for bonsai maintenance, designed for particular tasks, but they are not essential.

Right: A basic selection of bonsai tools. Top (left to right), tweezers, chopstick, wire brush, root hook. Bottom (left to right), concave branch cutter, trimming shears, long handled shears, wire cutters, pliers.

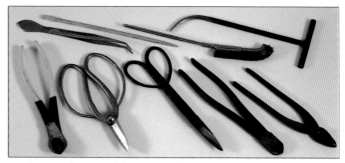

Generally speaking, any clean sharp instruments will suffice, although using the correct tools intended for the job does make life a little easier. Manufactured from high grade steel in Japan, cutters and implements are available at most bonsai centres to enable us to perform almost every imaginable styling and maintenance operation for bonsai cultivation.

Such a vast array of equipment, which might range from a simple chop-stick to a chainsaw is not only very expensive, but quite daunting to the novice. Since here we are only dealing with routine maintenance, a basic selection of bonsai tools is illustrated, which have been used during the production of this book.

Below: Finishing touches on wiring a Japanese larch group (Larix leptolepsis) and hornbeam (Carpinus betulus).

Below: A selction of coated aluminium bonsai wire.

Bottom: Bonsai look equally attractive on a frosty autumn morning.

Training wire is specially manufactured for bonsai styling and is also available at bonsai centres. Traditionally, annealed copper wire has been used but in recent years the more popular is copper coloured aluminium, which is softer and easier to use. Although flexible and easy to apply, the correct gauge of aluminium wire when coiled around trunks and branches is strong enough to allow repositioning. It is obtainable in various sizes from one to six millimetres in diameter.

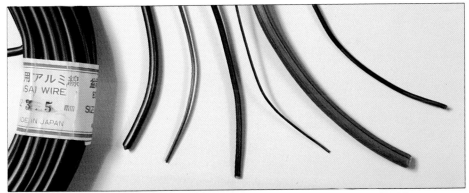

Above: Japanese maple (Acer palmatum linear-lobum).

Right: The author trimming needles on mountain pine (Pinus mugo).

Those of us who have given a few years of our lives to the cultivation of bonsai will be familiar with that joy of seeing trees provide regular seasonal displays. Working on our trees, styling and maintaining them, we constantly learn more and more of the fascinating charms of nature. In this respect we are all beginners. Every day we gain more knowledge, yet discover there is even more to understand. It is hoped that the wealth of experience that has lead to the production of the Bonsai Year Book, will guide and encourage you to bring out the best in your trees, each month, each season, year after year.

Below: Juniper (Juniperus chinensis var. pfitzeriana).

Below right: English elm (Ulmus procera).

THE
BONSAI
YEAR BOOK

SPRING

This maple (Acer japonicum aconitifolium)
displays beautiful tiny spring flowers
prior to leafing out.

Spring is often recognised among bonsai enthusiasts as being one of the busiest times of the year. Trees emerging from winter dormancy will need protection for tender new growth. The oncoming spring months will bring hazards of high winds, sudden downpours and late frosts. But for all of these problems, spring is an exciting time, with flushes of bright new colour in flowers and foliage.

SPRING

As the sap rises but before the buds break open is a good time to wire deciduous bonsai as it is difficult to wire through emerging buds or young leaves without damaging them. Wiring done before root-pruning and repotting will be easier as the tree is more stable; after wiring is completed it is easier to achieve the correct potting angle and placement in the container. On subjects suitable for leaf pruning in early to midsummer, a preferable time for wiring would be immediately after defoliation.

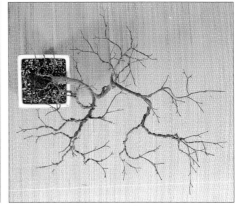

Top: Wiring Hornbeam (Carpinus betulus) before buds open.

Above: Wiring Japanese maple (Acer palmatum) and above right looking down showing how the branches are spread for even light.

This is an ideal month for repotting, particularly deciduous varieties but not spring flowering species such as azaleas, winter jasmine,quince etc. - wait until after flowering.

Soil compositions vary slightly with the requirements of individual tree species, for instance loamy soil is good for most deciduous trees, but pines require faster drainage. Azaleas and other lime hating species need an ericaceous mixture, yet some junipers thrive on a little lime in the drainage layer.

Generally speaking a good all round mix would be composed of one part loam; two parts moss peat (peat moss U.S.A.); two parts coarse grit.

Repotting and root pruning are carried out to enable pot bound plants to receive a fresh supply of soil and nutrients and to create the space for fresh new roots to grow. Young trees up to 10-15 years may need repotting every two to three years, but check first. Mature trees over 20 years may only need repotting every five years.

Right: Japanese maple (Acer palmatum) wiring prior to repotting.

Below: Cut the "tying in" wires.
Centre: Carefully remove the tree from the pot.
Right: Use a hook or rake to untangle the roots.

Cut any "tying in" wires underneath the pot and carefully remove the tree avoiding excessive root damage. With a hook or a rake gradually comb out the roots and roughly undo the tangled mass. Clean sharp scissors should be used to cut the long roots which have coiled around the inside of the pot. Then having raked out the old soil, cut the roots down to approximately half the original mass, making sure to remove any that are dead or decaying.

Right: Use clean, sharp scissors to cut the roots.

Far right: The reduced root ball.

Above: The pot is cleaned and prepared with drainage mesh, "tying in"wires, and a layer of coarse grit.

Above right: The tree is settled on to a layer of potting mixture.

The tree is then ready to return to its pot or a more suitable one if desired. Prepare the pot by placing some mesh over the drainage holes. Pass some wire through the drainage holes to tie the tree into position. A layer of coarse grit should then be used as a drainage layer. A layer of the potting mixture is placed over the grit to settle the tree in position. Tie the wires over the roots to stabilise the tree, but do not damage or crush the roots. Add the potting mixture, gently teasing in between the spread roots with a chopstick. Do not compress the soil, it needs to remain open for drainage.

Right: The "tying in"wires are firmly tightened over the roots.

Far right: Use a chopstick to tease the potting mixture in between the roots to avoid large air pockets.

Thoroughly water the tree and when the excess has drained off, add your chosen top dressing ie, moss, fine grit, or granular clay (Akadama), see appendix.

Newly potted trees need a degree of aftercare and protection. Shelter from wind and rain - only water when the soil shows signs of drying. Do not feed newly potted trees for about one month to six weeks. Do not place the tree in continued direct sunlight until new growth is evident.

Above: Thoughtful choice of soil dressing helps to set the mood.

Right: Repotting completed.

Below: Remove wire by cutting the coils.

Early season feeding for evergreens not newly potted may begin, but only a light application once this month. Do not feed trees in flower.

Trees that were wired last year whose branches are now set in the desired position may have the wires removed before buds open on deciduous species. Check to see if the wires are cutting in and be careful not to damage the new buds.

Delicate and fine twigged species will need protection from late frosts as the new leaves emerge, especially maple varieties.

TASKS IN BRIEF

Wiring may commence on deciduous trees.

Remove wire that was applied last year if branches have set or if wires are beginning to cut in.

Repot and root prune bonsai, but not spring flowering species.

Commence feeding evergreen trees not recently repotted.

Commence feeding deciduous trees if they show signs of activity, but not those recently repotted.

Shelter newly potted trees from the sun, wind, rain and frost.

Protect delicate and spring flowering trees from late frosts.

YEAR 1

YEAR 2	YEAR 3	YEAR 4

Continue to provide frost protection for newly emerging buds and leaves. If leaves suffer from frost burn before the new leaf buds have developed, some branches may die back and spoil the designed profile of the tree.

Right: Newly emerging leaves on delicate species such as this Japanese maple (Acer palmatum) need protection from frost and wind.

Below: Spring flowers on cherry (Prunus pissardii).

Shelter newly potted trees from excessive direct sun, wind and rain.

Do not feed trees in flower or newly potted trees. Wait until about six weeks after repotting.

Flowers on bonsai - particularly azaleas and wisteria, will last longer if sheltered from rain and overhead watering.

Rotate trees for even light to avoid strong directional growth of new shoots.

This is a good time to repot pines. Remember that pines benefit from extra grit in the potting mixture to aid drainage.

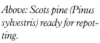

Above: Scots pine (Pinus sylvestris) ready for repotting.

Above centre: First cut the "tying in" wires.

Above right: An abundance of mycelium is revealed as the healthy tree is removed from its pot.

Do not be alarmed by the presence of a white fungus known as Mycelium found among the roots of healthy pines. The pine and the fungus have a symbiotic relationship which is beneficial to the health of the tree. To encourage its development, transfer a little of the soil and fungus to the new potting mixture.

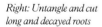

Right: Untangle and cut long and decayed roots

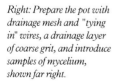

Right: Prepare the pot with drainage mesh and "tying in" wires, a drainage layer of coarse grit, and introduce samples of mycelium, shown far right.

Notice here that the position of the tree has been moved to the right to achieve better harmony between tree and pot.

Top: Place a layer of potting mixture over the drainage grit to settle the tree, then firmly but carefully tie the tree into position.

Top right: A chopstick is used to tease the mixture in between the roots.

Above: Potting mixture for pines may often consist of up to 70% grit to aid drainage.

Right: The soil surface is neatly dressed with Akadama clay, and the exercise is complete.

Feeding routines may get under way on established trees. One application should be sufficient this month. Use a liquid foliar feed on deciduous trees and a slow release granular fertiliser for pines. Refer to appendix for feeding details.

Right: Slow release granular feeding for pines. Shown here mountain pine (Pinus mugo).

Below: Strip the bark off unwanted branches to create jin.

Careful monitoring of water on established bonsai will affect the amount of new growth. Too much water will cause long sappy shoot extensions on deciduous trees, thus losing any fine twiggy detail that has already been achieved. Pines and other needled evergreens will suffer from long large needles which will result in heavy branches instead of delicate tips, particularly at the apex.

This is a good time to strip bark for jin and shari, the contrived deadwood areas which creates an aged appearance. Bark stripping at this time will allow the wood to dry in preparation for lime sulphur application in the summer.

TASKS IN BRIEF

Protect delicate trees from frost.

Shelter newly potted trees.

Feeding schedules may commence but do not feed newly potted trees or trees in flower.

Avoid rain or water contact on flowers.

Rotate trees for even light.

Repot pines.

Monitor and restrict amount of water to retain fine detail.

YEAR 1

YEAR 2	YEAR 3	YEAR 4

Late frosts can still be a problem during this month, so protection is advisable for delicate species. Prolonged periods of full sun together with wind can be problematical particularly for maples. The leaves may scorch and look a little unsightly. Continue to rotate trees for even light to avoid growth in one direction.

Above: Tender young maple leaves are easily damaged by frost contact.

Right: Japanese Maple (Acer palmatum 'Deshojo') displaying spectacular spring foliage.

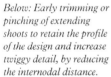

Feeding should now be increased to twice a month for trees not recently repotted or root pruned. Evergreens, particularly pines, may benefit by alternating between liquid and granular applications.

Watch out for wires cutting in on rapid growth; remove if necessary - be careful of new leaves and buds. Remove the wire by cutting the coils rather than trying to uncoil the wire.

Trim long shoots on deciduous trees retaining the silhouette of the bonsai, unless you particularly need branch extension at any location on the tree.

As they fade remove dead flowers from azaleas, rhododendron and other early flowering trees .

Below: Early trimming or pinching of extending shoots to retain the profile of the design and increase twiggy detail, by reducing the internodal distance.

Varieties which flowered early in spring including quince and winter jasmine should be pruned, shaped and wired. A good time to repot these species is immediately after flowering.

Regulate the amount of water for pines to govern the size of new needles. Too much will encourage long candles producing large needles, which are undesirable unless the tree is being forced to gain bulk. Give just enough water to maintain healthy trees.

Finger pinch or cut soft growth on larch to desired length. This will promote clusters of buds at the base of the new shoots.

Right: The brilliant soft green foliage of Japanese larch (Larix leptolepsis) in spring.

Right: Trim the growth extension to just beyond a bud. Select a bud facing in the direction of required new growth.

Far right: The effect of prolonged exposure to hot sun on fresh new larch growth can result in scorch. Notice that cones form easily on larch bonsai.

Vigorous junipers will require occasional finger pinching to keep the new growth compact. As the new season's growth gets under way, junipers can very quickly become a dense mass of foliage resembling a mop rather than a dwarf tree. Weeds will also rapidly infest the soil at this time so it is important not to let the situation get out of control and rob the bonsai of valuable nutrients.

Above: Common juniper (Juniperus communis) thinning and trimming to retrieve the basic design.

Now that the cold wet weather is well behind us, it is good practice to clean off grime and algae that build up throughout the winter months. Gentle brushing with a toothbrush and water on deciduous trunks should be sufficient. Take care not to damage buds when brushing. Wire brushing on juniper trunks brings out red pigmentation in the bark which contrasts nicely with any whitened deadwood areas. Do not brush through to the white sap wood layer, be careful not to overdo it. It is not advisable to treat pines in this way particularly where flaky plates of bark need to be retained.

Right: Toothbrush and water scrub on elm trunk.

Far right: Gentle wire brushing brings out red pigmentation in juniper bark.

Be alert to pests and diseases; warm damp conditions cause mildew. Check for a white chalky deposit on the underside of broad leaves. This is the early stage of the condition and can be controlled with a proprietary systemic fungicide. Susceptible species including oak, hawthorn, crab apple and beech are best sprayed as the buds are swelling and at regular intervals thereafter. See appendix.

Below: Mildew on oak leaves.

Below right: Woolly aphid in pine needles.

Aphids gather on the underside of broadleaves particularly on beech and crab apple. Woolly aphids are often identified as small cotton wool like clusters at the base of needles usually in pines, larch and sometimes on crab apple. Systemic insecticides should control most aphid and insect attacks. Use caution when applying sprays, they can cause irritation to the skin and eyes, do not inhale, always refer to manufacturers instructions. Leaves are likely to scorch if sprayed in full sunshine.

Right: Aphids - Greenfly; Blackfly; Whitefly.

TASKS IN BRIEF

Protect tender trees from late frosts.

Protect tender trees from excess sun.

Rotate all trees for even light.

Feed trees not recently repotted or root pruned with a balanced fertiliser.

Monitor any wires which may be cutting in and remove accordingly.

Trim or pinch out long shoots.

Remove dead flowers.

Repot flowering species after flowers have died.

Ensure adequate watering.

Regulate watering for pines.

Clean trunks of bonsai.

Check for pests and diseases and treat accordingly.

YEAR 1

YEAR 2	YEAR 3	YEAR 4

THE
BONSAI
YEAR BOOK

SUMMER

*Japanese maple (Acer palmatum) shows its
vivid summer brilliance in a
formal display setting.*

By now, all bonsai should be in their display position in the garden. They should be located above ground on tables, staging or poles to receive even sunlight, good ventilation and easy access for maintenance. Some light shade may be beneficial together with protection from strong prevailing winds.

SUMMER

Early summer is time to consider the detailed structuring of pines, which can be influenced by selective pinching of new candles as they emerge. Ensure that the pine is healthy and well fed before commencing this work. Lower branches are usually weaker and less vigorous than upper regions of the tree, so to alter this balance, the pinching procedure is best phased over a period of time.

Below: Scots pine (Pinus sylvestris) three tree planting.

For two needled varieties, the lower weaker regions should be tackled first. This will stimulate new bud production within these areas and provide a head start over the stronger upper portion of the tree, which should be treated in the same manner about two weeks later. The result is that by the end of the season, the balance and distribution of new buds and needle size will be more even throughout the tree. Excessive numbers of buds which may appear in the apex as a result of this technique may be selectively removed to further aid the balance, preventing the tree from becoming top heavy.

Right: Candle pinching two needle varieties (Japanese black pine)

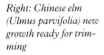

Above: Candle pinching five needle varieties (Japanese white pine).

When the new candles reach approximately one inch in length and before the needles emerge from the shoot, pinch out a proportion of the candles. **Caution**. While it may be possible to remove the candle in full on two needle pines, i.e. scots pine, black pine, mugo pine etc., one should never remove more than two thirds of each candle on five needle varieties such as white pine. Reverse the procedure for white pine, tackling the upper vigorous regions first.

Continue to feed all trees except for summer flowering varieties including satsuki azaleas. Evergreens prefer a alternating schedule between granular and liquid foliar feeding every two weeks. Mature aged specimens will require less feed than young bonsai being forced to gain bulk. See appendix on feeding. Deciduous trees will be growing quite rapidly by now so continue trimming back long shoots. Trim the shoot to just above a bud which faces in the direction of required new growth.

Right: Chinese elm (Ulmus parvifolia) new growth ready for trimming

Far right: Japanese maple (Acer palmatum) trimming new growth.

Above: Field maple (Acer campestre) leaf removal procedure.

Leaf removal may be carried out on some deciduous trees this month. This is most effective on species that have successive flushes of growth i.e. maples, elm, birch, hornbeam etc., but species such as oak and beech should be treated with caution. Cut the leaf petioles with clean, sharp scissors to remove the leaves. After two or three weeks the new buds will swell to produce a new crop of leaves. The result will be more numerous smaller leaves, better branch detail and ramification, together with more vivid autumn colour. In extreme hot conditions, some mist spraying will be beneficial. Trees grown for flowers or fruit should not be leaf pruned.

Below: Finger pinching spruce.

Right: Finger pinching juniper new growth.

Trees that have been leaf pruned are best wired at this time as the branches and twigs are more flexible than in winter or spring. It is easier to style the tree without crowded foliage to contend with.

This month is a suitable time to repot azaleas after flowering and perhaps even later for satsuki varieties.

Right: Satsuki azalea, (Kaho) in full flower. Wait until after flowering before repotting.

Continue to look for insect attacks particularly aphids on the underside of broad leaves, especially beech. Woolly aphids and scale can also be a problem. All the above should be treated with systemic insecticide. Mildew may also be present if ventilation is poor. Treat trees most likely to be affected i.e. hawthorn, oak, crab apple, beech and maple. Systemic fungicide is suitable to control the problem, but if it advances to a black sooty mould on trunk and branches, it will need brushing or scraping off. In very severe cases it may be necessary to remove the affected branch.

Right: Scale insects appear on trunks.

Far right: Mildew on oak leaves.

Right: Bonsai in summer display position.

Below: Delicate species may be placed under the staging to protect from excessive direct summer sun.

Many broadleaf species will benefit from some protection from hot summer sun, particularly in the afternoon. Maples and yew grow better in partial shade but expect some loss of colour on maple leaves.

Larch may need trimming back by the end of this month. Trim to desired length just beyond a bud. Select a bud that is facing in the direction of desired new growth.

Wire that has been left on branches too long and has bitten into the bark is best removed during the height of the growing season. Cut the coils rather than try to unwind the wire. Any damage caused by removing the wire causes scar tissue to grow, and rapid healing helps to disguise wire marks.

Right: Wire biting into pine. Cut the coils rather than attempt to unwind the wire.

Generally speaking, unless the tree has suffered severe strangulation, wire marks are only regarded as being superficial, and will grow out. For pines and vigorous growing evergreens this should take two or three seasons. Smooth bark trees such as maple and beech may take a little longer. In any event, it is not usually detrimental to the health of the tree.

Below: Remove flowers as they fade on azaleas.

Flowering trees which have produced blooms earlier in the year may now be pruned. Cut back to within the flowering regions of the tree retaining sufficient nodes to produce shoots and flowers next year. Feed may be given to flowering varieties after flowers have faded and the heads removed. Use a balanced feed until autumn. Remember that rhododendrons will require an ericaceous fertiliser. Fruiting trees such as crab apple should not be fed until the fruit has set. New vegetative growth may be forced and cause the fruit to drop.

TASKS IN BRIEF

Selectively pinch out pine candles.

Feed all trees (except for summer flowering varieties), with a balanced fertiliser.

Trim long growth on deciduous trees.

Pinch out extending shoots on evergreens.

Defoliate or carry out leaf removal on appropriate deciduous trees.

Wire those trees which have been defoliated.

Repot azaleas after flowering.

Check for pests and diseases and treat accordingly.

Protect delicate trees from hot afternoon sun.

Prune trees which flowered earlier.

Water all trees thoroughly.

YEAR 1

YEAR 2	YEAR 3	YEAR 4

Partial shade may be necessary during extreme heat for delicate species, especially maples. High temperatures and wind may cause rapid drying and cause roots to burn in shallow pots. Keep up humidity under these circumstances or shade trees from direct overhead afternoon sun. Trees may need watering several times daily on exposed sites.

Below: Japanese maple (Acer palmatum roseomarginatum). The delicate beauty of this tree is the result of thoughtful care and protection from extremes of weather.

Watering technique is important. Always use a fine rose on a hose or watering can. Never blast high pressure water at the tree or soil. Water thoroughly until water runs from the drainage holes. Wait until just before the soil is dry before watering again. Tap water is acceptable but rain water is better.

Continue to rotate the trees or move them around the site to avoid prominent growth in one direction.

Some glaucous species of evergreens which include white pines, cedars, some junipers and spruces display a deeper richer colour if given some shade.

Right: Japanese white pine (Pinus parviflora) displaying blue/green needles.

Maintain feeding schedules twice a month for all trees. Liquid foliar feeding (drenching) may be used for deciduous bonsai, but some growers report leaf burn problems if carried out in mid afternoon sun. Alternate between liquid drenching and granular feed for pines. Never over feed, refer to manufacturers instructions - see appendix.

Pines and fruit bearing trees may benefit from a drenching of Epsom salts to boost the intake of magnesium and iron, particularly if the leaves appear too yellow.

Right: Liquid foliar feeding.

Far right: Slow release granular feeding.

Continue to check for pests hiding underneath leaves, at the base of needles or in bark crevices. Treat with a proprietary systemic insecticide.

Throughout the growing season, trim back overlong new growth on deciduous bonsai to retain the designed silhoutte of the tree. Trimming also encourages back buds to break and develop a more detailed and twiggy structural skeleton.

Below: Trimming deciduous new growth; left - oak; centre - Chinese elm; right - hornbeam.

During the height of the season many vigorous growing trees become so dense and compact that the bonsai quickly loses its shape and basic design. Bonsai like all plants continue to grow, constantly evolving, so we must always monitor and keep new growth in check. Allow branches to extend where required to improve thc design, and cut back to retain balance. Dense crowded foliage can cause inner branches and foliage to die due to lack of light and poor ventilation.

Below: Chinese juniper (Juniperus chinensis Blaauws variety) in need of thinning out.

Below right: Looking up into the dense mass.

Juniper varieties often fall victim to dense congested branches due to thorough pinching regimes and good feeding schedules.

Their response to pinching make junipers ideal subjects for bonsai. The accompanying photographs illustrate maintenance trimming on Chinese juniper (Blaauws variety). No wiring is used at this time, just thinning out and pinching back extended shoots. Scissor cut twigs and stems but only finger pinch green foliage to avoid browning of tips.

Right: Trimming and thinning completed

.

Far right: Looking up into the branches after thinning out.

The aim is to improve separation between the main branches and to open up the structure of the tree. This allows light and air into the interior while creating the image of a mature tree rather than a dense bush or mop. Notice also that the trunk has been cleaned and brushed to bring out natural red pigmentation.

Right: The exercise completed .

TASKS IN BRIEF

Protect delicate trees from prolonged sun.

Water all trees thoroughly.

Rotate trees for even light.

Maintain feeding with balanced feed.

Check for pests and treat accordingly.

Trim deciduous trees.

Thin out and reduce overcrowding in dense evergreen branches.

YEAR 1

YEAR 2	YEAR 3	YEAR 4

Growth will be slowing down this month so reduce feed applications. Deciduous bonsai should be fed with a zero nitrogen "drench" so as not to force unwanted sappy growth this late in the season. Feed just once in this month.

Pines and other evergreens may be fed just once with a zero nitrogen feed or even omit feeding for this month.

Below: Juniper (Chinensis San Josè) growing on artificially carved rock standing in suiban (shallow water tray).

Rock plantings will need protection from extreme heat. Increase humidity by standing in or over a water tray to prevent drying. Willows and water loving trees will benefit if stood in a shallow tray of water.

This time of year can still provide some very hot days so be prepared to shelter delicate broadleaf species as required. Although growth is reduced, heat and wind will still dry out the soil, so keep a check on watering.

Right: Willow (Salix alba) requires copious amounts of water during summer months, shown here standing permanently in tray of water.

For pines, any candles that were allowed free growth throughout the season, may be cut back during this month. Trim the portion of new growth with sharp

Right: Cutting into current season's growth on two needle pine variety.

Far right: The effect of earlier candle pinching causes bud production among the needles, likewise in the following spring after August trimming.

scissors back to the desired length. This will assist in the production of new buds among existing needles. Try to avoid cutting through the needles when you cut the shoot.

Coniferous trees such as pine and larch will occasionally produce cones after flowers have pollinated. While they do look attractive, an overabundance can draw too much energy from the plant and weaken lower regions of the tree. The presence of cones - usually in the apex - causes supporting branches to thicken thus spoiling fine detailed structure. Be alert to the situation and remove any or all if they appear to be causing a problem. Always use a wound sealant when cutting pines, excessive loss of resin will weaken the plant.

Right: Cones developing on Japanese white pine.

Far right: End of season trimming for cedar.

End of season trimming can be carried out on most species later this month. Long branches which have grown beyond the designed proportions of the tree should be cut back to retain the desired shape. Be cautious when trimming flowering trees, retain those areas which are likely to produce blooms next spring.

Below: Dwarf honeysuckle (Lonicera nitida) before and after trimming.

Remove some fruit from overladen trees. Not only can the weight of many crab apples and cherries bend and sometimes break branches on smaller bonsai, the burden of developing fruit draws a large amount of energy from the plant and may weaken the bonsai.

Wiring may be carried out on small branches before the wood becomes too hard. Be careful not to damage the buds at the base of leaves as these will emerge as new smaller branches next year.

A lime sulphur application on deadwood features may be beneficial while the days are still quite hot and dry. This not only bleaches the wood but also helps to prevent decay through the oncoming damp months. Ensure that the application has thoroughly dried before exposing to rain or misting. Water the soil only, for a few days to avoid washing the mixture off. See appendix.

Below: Lime sulphur application to deadwood areas.

As was mentioned at the beginning of this book we are dealing with outdoor trees, although they can be brought indoors for display, but for no longer than three to four days at a time. However if you're cultivating several specimens, its possible to arrange a permanent display area where you can always have one of your trees indoors on show.

Right: A typical Japanese style display area (Tokonoma in Japanese).

TASKS IN BRIEF

Reduce or alter feeding schedule. Use low or zero nitrogen fertiliser

Keep up watering.

Protect delicate trees and rock plantings from extreme heat.

Trim back current season's growth on pines where candles were not pinched out earlier.

Trim back overlong new growth on all trees.

Remove some fruit from overladen trees.

Wire current season's growth that requires postioning.

Remove any wires cutting into bark.

Apply lime sulphur solution where required.

YEAR 1

YEAR 2	YEAR 3	YEAR 4

THE
BONSAI
YEAR BOOK

AUTUMN

This stately English elm (Ulmus procera) annually produces this golden autumn display.

Autumn is a season of change. Late hot spells can lead us into false security. Sudden early frosts or periods of prolonged rain will cause problems later if we are not prepared.

Deciduous bonsai that have been well fed will provide us with magnificent displays of autumn colours and hues. Deep fiery reds on maples to shimmering golds on birches and elms make our seasons efforts so rewarding.

AUTUMN

The early part of this month is still a suitable time for trimming back growth on pines. Old needles on pines turn yellow before dropping, there is no need for alarm. Remove the old needles by hand, they come off quite easily.

Thin out the previous years needles and current season's growth, to allow light and ventilation into the tree. Where denser growth is required, scissor cut the needles leaving the sheath which retains them. For neatness, trim off all downward growing needles and wire the branches into flat spreading pads, to allow an even light to reach all the new buds.

Above: Removing old needles, trimming and re-wiring Japanese white pine (Pinus parviflora)

Right: Major cuts on pines should be treated with a wound sealant to prevent "bleeding" and fungal entry.

Reduced activity in bonsai at this time of year is reflected in the plants water requirements - do not over water. Some overhead protection may be required from heavy autumn rainfall. There is a risk of root rot, particularly with deciduous bonsai if they spend dormant winter months in soaking wet soil.

Below: Berberis in autumn colour.

A feed application containing no nitrogen is beneficial during this month, not to promote growth, but to harden the current seasons growth and strengthen buds for the oncoming winter. It would not be desirable to promote excessive new growth at this time, for it would not mature in time for winter and will only die back later. Also it would be disastrous to allow toxic nitrogen build up in the soil for those trees approaching dormancy.

Emergency repotting of weak and sickened trees may be carried out if absolutely necessary, but oncoming winter protection will be required. Keep any repotted trees cool to prevent new growth. Do not feed.

Fruit bearing bonsai may need protection from birds, they will strip attractive coloured berries in no time.

Above: Autumn fruit on pyracantha.

Above right: Early autumn colour on trident maple (Acer buergerianum).

Remove wire on branches that are now set in the desired position. This is probably the last month in the season to carry out new wiring on delicate species that become brittle during the dormant winter months. Berberis is a good example, branches are easily broken if wiring is attempted late in the year.

Early winter protection may be required for some delicate semi-tropical species such as pomegranate.

TASKS IN BRIEF

Trim growth and remove old needles on pines.

Reduce watering.

Feed trees with a low or zero nitrogen fertiliser.

Protect fruits from birds.

Remove any wires cutting into bark.

Wire new growth into desired position.

Protect delicate species from early frosts.

YEAR 1

YEAR 2	YEAR 3	YEAR 4

Reduce water for all trees. Avoid the soil becoming soaking wet for oncoming winter.

One application of feed without nitrogen may be given to all trees this month. Do not encourage unwanted late growth. Do not feed any newly potted trees.

Above: Japanese maple (Acer palmatum) provide fabulous autumn displays.

Right: Notice the autumn gold of European larch (Larix decidua). Notice also the presence of cones.

Trees that were wired at the beginning of the season may now need the wire removed. For deciduous species, it is better to wait until the leaves have fallen. Pruning and shaping deciduous trees is easier once the leaves have fallen. Use a wound sealant on any large cuts to prevent fungal entry. Wiring may be carried out to set the current season's growth, naturally it is more effective if done before the wood hardens. Some delicate species may react with heavy wiring during extreme cold, so be cautious and be prepared for winter protection.

Below: End of season trimming and wiring Japanese maple (Acer palmatum roseomarginatum).

Right: Pines may be thinned and wired at this time.

Below: Bright red berries on cotoneaster may need protection from birds.

Any emergency repotting will need shelter and protection, make sure the plants are not kept too wet.

Continue to remove old yellow needles from pines. Keep pot surfaces free from falling leaves on all trees. The collecting debris may harbour pests and fungi during damp months.

Continue to protect fruit and berries from hungry birds.

Flowering trees may be given a high potassium fertiliser every two weeks during this month to set and strengthen the flower buds for next season's blooms.

Mid autumn is a suitable time to repot and root prune pines and evergreens. If carried out now there should be sufficient time for rehabilitation before the onset of winter.

If necessary select and prepare a more suitable pot, using some drainage mesh and "tying in" wires. The juniper shown in the example has not been repotted for at least three years and may very well be pot bound. It may also be more suited to a shallower oval instead of the deep squat angular pot that it has been growing in.

Any styling by pruning or wiring should be completed before the repotting procedure, while the tree is stable in its pot. **Caution.** Pines may suffer if drastic pruning and root pruning are carried out in the same growing season.

Right: Juniper Chinensis San José in preparation for repotting.

Below: Bonsai are usually secured in their pots with wire which passes through the drainage holes. Cut any "tying in" wires before attempting to remove the tree from its pot.

Cut the "tying in" wires and gently remove the tree. Using a hook or similar implement untangle the mass of roots and tease out much of the old soil.

Below and right:
Reducing the tangle of old
roots.

Use sharp scissors to make clean cuts through the roots, removing one third to half depending on the health and vigour of the tree. Also remove any roots that are dead or have rotted through neglect.

Prepare the new pot with drainage mesh and "tying in" wire. Place a layer of coarse grit to enhance the drainage in the bottom of the new pot. Then add a suitable depth of potting mixture, see appendix.

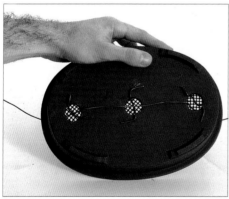

Above: Preparing the new pot with drainage mesh and "tying in" wire.

Above right: A base layer of coarse grit is used to improve drainage.

The tree is secured into position with the "tying in" wires. Do not overtighten the wire, causing damage to the roots, but only sufficient to stabilise the tree. The ideal planting position is slightly to one side of the pot, and when looking down from above, a little to the rear of centre.

Spread the roots radially if possible from the trunk and add further potting mixture, teasing into the root system with a wooden chopstick. Do not compress the mixture, fast drainage is important. Do not stab and fracture the roots.

Right: The tree is carefully tied into position.

Below: Potting mixture is added with the aid of a chopstick.

Below right: Moss is placed on the surface to enhance the mood.

Give the planting a good soaking with a fine rose on a watering can, to settle the mixture. Finally, dress the surface with mosses, gravel or Akadama clay soil.

Right: The exercise completed. The tree looks more suited to its new pot.

Aftercare is always important when repotting bonsai. Water will not be required until the planting begins drying out through its own activity, shelter should be provided. Do not feed trees repotted in autumn until there are signs of activity in the following season.

TASKS IN BRIEF

Reduce watering.

Feed with high potash fertiliser.

Remove any wires biting into bark.

Prune and shape deciduous trees after leaf fall.

Remove old needles from pines.

Protect fruit from birds.

Feed flowering trees with high potassium fertiliser.

Evergreens may be repotted, do not feed newly potted trees.

YEAR 1

YEAR 2	YEAR 3	YEAR 4

Generally speaking, do not feed trees this month - but some evergreens in development may benefit from one light application of a balanced fertiliser.

Protect trees, particularly dormant deciduous species, from excess rainfall. Do not allow soils to become water-logged.

Right: White willow (Salix alba) after end of season trimming.

Branches on deciduous trees will be too brittle now for wiring, but shaping by pruning can be carried out. Be sure to use a wound sealant on cuts to prevent entry of fungus during damp winter months. When leaves have fallen it is so much easier to analyse the structure of deciduous trees, so any major alterations are best carried out during these months.

Remove any remaining leaves on deciduous trees, and from soil surfaces, they may harbour overwintering pests and insects.

Above: Always use a wound sealant on large cuts.

Above right: The structural cascade of this European larch (Larix decidua) is revealed when the leaves have fallen.

Beech and some oak varieties retain old brown leaves during winter. This helps to protect next years buds; there is no cause for alarm. Protection will now be required for delicate semi-tropical species, trees in shallow pots and on rocks, and those with fleshy roots, i.e. Chinese elm, trident maple, Gingko, yew etc.

Right: Fleshy root varieties such as this yew (Taxus baccata) may need protection from severe frost .

Below: Frost contact will damage flower buds on azaleas.

Guard azaleas from early frosts, otherwise the flower buds may fail in the new season.

TASKS IN BRIEF

Do not feed (except trees in development).

Shelter trees from excess rainfall.

Remove dead leaves and keep soil surfaces clean.

Prune trees as required.

Protect delicate and semi-tropical species from early frost.

YEAR 1

YEAR 2	YEAR 3	YEAR 4

THE
BONSAI
YEAR BOOK

WINTER

This juniper , a cultivar of Juniperus virginiana is happy to tolerate mild winter weather.

Bonsai in winter dormancy offer a time of contemplation. Leafless trees can be studied in detail, major pruning can be carried out and plans made for detailed wiring in the new season. Soils and potting mixtures should be prepared, and more appropriate pots selected where required. Winter is also a time for gaining inspiration and learning from trees growing in the wild.

WINTER

Pruning trees may still be carried out this month but do not attempt bending and wiring dormant deciduous bonsai, branches become surprisingly brittle when the sap is not flowing.

Right: Crab apple (Malus Professor Sprenger) will often retain fruit after leaf fall.

Guard bonsai from freezing winds, evergreens may suffer from burn or discolouration if they cannot take up moisture when the soil is frozen. Some species such as juniper and cryptomeria, change colour and appear burnt or dessicated. This reaction to cold is quite natural, do not be alarmed, colours will revert to normal deep greens early in the new season when temperatures start to rise.

This month is not normally too hard on bonsai, but prepare for cold January and February with appropriate shelter.

If bonsai are brought indoors for display, do so for only for three to four days and keep away from heat, thus avoiding any possibility of encouraging new growth.

Above right: The effect of winter cold on cryptomeria.

Above: Juniper may also change colour during severe cold spells, but soon reverts to normal colour when temperatures rise in the spring as shown below.

Right: Japanese elm (Zelkova serrata)

Above: Gain inspiration from mature trees in the wild. English oak.

Do not feed bonsai this month and avoid too much water. Dormant trees may suffer root rot if kept too wet.

It is easier to evaluate the design and branch placement of deciduous bonsai during the leafless period.

TASKS IN BRIEF

Prune trees as required.

Shelter from excess rainfall.

Protect from freezing wind and exposed areas.

Do not feed trees.

Clean dead leaves and debris from soil surfaces.

YEAR 1

YEAR 2	YEAR 3	YEAR 4

Above: The realism of a distant copse is created by this group of stewartia (Stewartia monodelpha).

Protect evergreens from winter winds. Trees are not normally harmed if the soil is frozen, but wind will burn and dry out the foliage if the plant cannot take up water. Azaleas and broad leaved evergreens including pyracantha and buxus will benefit from such protection.

Right: Those bonsai which benefit from winter protection may be placed under display staging, which is then wrapped with plastic sheeting.

Guard bonsai from being kept too wet to avoid the possibility of root rot.

Keep bonsai away from heat and direct sunlight through glass if brought indoors. Warmth will spur new growth cycles into action which will die off and cause the plant irreparable harm when returned to normal cooler temperatures. Do not bring outdoor bonsai into the home for more than three to four days.

Right: Purple beech (Fagus sylvatica purpurea) retain old leaves through the winter.

Above: Naturally contorted trees offer great inspiration for bonsai styling.

Below and right: Emulating nature with variegated juniper (Juniperus alba variegata).

Do not feed bonsai, and continue to shelter from excess water. Trees not benefiting from winter protection may suffer from excessive weight of snow on delicate branches, so be alert to this situation. Bonsai always look quite charming after a light snowfall, but remember that evergreens will retain quite a weight of snow on their branches, and if wired, may alter the design of the tree.

Study design and gain inspiration from trees in the wild.

TASKS IN BRIEF

Protect trees from freezing winds.

Shelter from excess rainfall or heavy snow.

Do not feed.

YEAR 1

YEAR 2	YEAR 3	YEAR 4

Some finely twigged deciduous trees, especially chinese elm, maples and birch, may suffer some twig die back during winter, so the end of this month is a good time to trim back and neaten the silhouette of these

Right: This majestic English elm (Ulmus procera) reveals its full winter grandeur.

Azaleas and other winter flowering trees will benefit if protected from freezing winds, flower production will be greater.

Below: Delicate species will require some protection from the worst of the winter weather.

Right: Needles on pines become brown and buds will weaken if kept too wet during winter. Ensure that the soil drains quickly.

Far right: Fine twigged species such as maples suffer some twig die back during winter.

Prepare potting mixtures for new season repotting and select new and more appropriate pots where necessary. The new season will become a very busy time, so be prepared. Some repotting of deciduous trees may begin now where heavy work loads are envisaged.

Below: A wide selection of pots are available at your bonsai centre.

Right: Sometimes junipers may display a purple/brown tinge in the depth of winter.

Far right: Continue to make comparisons with mature trees in the wild for inspiration in design and refinement.

During winter, bonsai may be brought indoors for display but only for three to four days. Keep away from heat and direct sunlight through glass.

Continue to restrict water. Do not feed deciduous trees, but those evergreens that are not destined for repotting may be given one light balanced feed.

TASKS IN BRIEF

Trim twigs and branches which have died back during cold spells.

Protect trees from freezing winds.

Avoid frost contact on winter flowering trees.

Prepare for repotting, new pots and potting mixtures.

Do not feed trees except evergreens not destined for repotting. Use a balanced fertiliser.

Shelter trees from excess rainfall and heavy snow.

YEAR 1

YEAR 2	YEAR 3	YEAR 4

*Above: European larch
(Larix decidua)*

*Right: English oak
(Quercus robur)*

FEEDING

Nutrient requirements for bonsai are provided by regular fertiliser applications. Never overfeed your trees. Small amounts given at regular intervals are far better than occasional heavy doses.

Never feed trees that have just been repotted or root pruned. Always allow 4 - 6 weeks after repotting to avoid damage to freshly cut root ends.

Fertilisers are given mainly during the growing season. For deciduous species, this begins at the sign of activity and opening of buds, usually during early spring. This may be in the form of a liquid foliar feed (drench), or granular feed given every two weeks until the end of summer. A generally available balanced feed of approximately equal proportions of Nitrogen/Phosphate/Potassium is ideal to promote lush growth. Drench the whole plant, but avoid foliage contact during hot summer afternoon sun. Never feed trees that are in flower.

During autumn give monthly applications of a high Potassium (Potash) fertiliser to harden current season's growth and strengthen buds in preparation for next season.

Do not feed deciduous trees during dormant winter months.

Evergreens may commence their feeding schedules about a month earlier at the end of winter, and terminate slightly later in the season, but as with deciduous trees, do not feed in the depth of winter.

Begin feeding just before spring activity with a balanced application of slow release granular type once a month. Then as spring gets under way, feed twice a month alternating with a liquid drench. Change to a high Potassium (Potash) fertiliser during autumn after which young trees being forced to gain bulk may be given a light final balanced feed before the onset of winter.

Mature trees of all types will require less feed than younger trees in developement, give them sufficient amounts to maintain health and vigour, without encouraging rampant shoot extensions.

Never feed bonsai that are in poor health due to unsuitable potting mixtures or bad drainage. Toxic nitrogen may build up in the soil and cause even more harm to the plant. Trees should not be fed when the soil has totally dried out. Dampen the soil first to avoid scorching the roots.

Apply liquid feed in acordance with manufacturers instructions. Use granular feeds sparingly.

LIME SULPHUR

Lime sulphur is, as its name suggests, a mixture of lime and sulphur boiled together. It is used in bonsai as a preservative agent on deadwood areas and enhances the natural appearance with a bleaching effect.

When the branch or deadwood areas are thoroughly dry, lime sulphur is applied with a brush. At first the yellow liquid may appear garish, but it turns white as it dries. Lime sulphur should be applied during dry summer months. Be careful not to splash the liquid on the soil or pot.

Lime sulphur is generally available at most bonsai centres.

POTTING MIXTURES

The requirement for bonsai potting mixtures is the ability to drain freely. Poor drainage will often result in lack of vigour or even sudden death of a bonsai.

Generally speaking a standard mixture would consist of one part loam; two parts peat; two parts coarse grit.

The quality of the peat should be long grained e.g. Sphagnum moss peat (known as peat moss U.S.A.). Grit should be 2 - 4 mm in size, and a mixture of smooth and coarse particles.

The ingredients are best mixed when dry, and fine particles should be sieved out.

The standard mixture is suitable for broadleaf species but pines benefit from a higher proportion of grit, even up to 70% of the mixture. In such cases loam may be replaced with a rotted leaf mould collected from below healthy pines. Junipers often prefer a few chips of limestone placed in the drainage layer. Remember that rhododendrons and other lime hating plants will need special consideration with an ericaceous mixture.

Small size bonsai less than 3 inches high may need less grit in the mixture and a smaller particle size. Washed horticultural sand would be suitable.

Akadama is a Japanese granular volcanic clay extensively used in Japan for potting most species. If available to you it is usable as a potting medium or alternatively as a surface dressing.

SYSTEMICS

Systemic insecticide and fungicides are used to assist in the control of many plant disorders experienced in bonsai.

The systemic is absorbed into the plant tissues and helps defend the plant from insect or fungus attack. It is more effective when used as a regular cautionary spray. Always refer to the manufacturer's instructions when using chemical applications. Do not inhale the spray and avoid contact with skin and eyes.

WIRING

Artistic shapes and designs are created in bonsai by selective pruning and wiring trunks and branches into desired posi-

tions. Copper coloured aluminium wire is manufactured specifically for bonsai training and is available at bonsai centres. The wire is produced in a variety of sizes from one to six millimetres in diameter. Select a suitable gauge for the branch in question, starting with heavy wires on larger branches first and progressing to finer wires for detailed styling. To be effective the wire must be firmly anchored in the soil at the base of the trunk, or around the trunk when two branches are wired with the same length of wire. The wire is coiled around the branch at an angle of about 45°, and the branch is then bent or moved into the desired position.

Never overtighten wires. Branches will continue to thicken as the growing season gets under way, therefore constant monitoring and removal of wire will avoid unsightly scars. Take extreme care when wiring through newly emerging buds and shoots, they may be easily damaged.

Neatness is important, and if wiring is executed correctly, should not impair the overall appearance of the tree.

CLIMATIC VARIATIONS

In compiling this book we have based the timing of the various tasks on the Northern Temperate regions i.e. Great Britain, most of Europe and most of the United States. Northerly regions such as Scandinavia, Alaska and Canada will have to make adjustments as will Southern regions such as the Southern Mediterranean, Southern states of the U.S.A. and Central America.

INDEX

INDEX

THE BONSAI YEAR BOOK

I am deeply grateful for the support and encouragement of Harry Tomlinson whose guidance from the outset of this project has turned the concept into reality.

Thank you also to Nigel Osborne for the valuable advice on production.

Special thanks go to Howard Fillingham for the Mac typesetting and page make up, for his tolerance in working to tight scheduling throughout the production of artwork, and for supplying copious amounts of whisky and strong coffee to keep us going.

Thank you also to the following for loaning trees for photography:-

Harry Tomlinson:
Front cover Satsuki azalea
Black pine
p.29 Deshojo maple
p.38 Japanese maple
p.39 Field maple
p.40 Satsuki azalea
p.54 Cedar in display
p.60 Trident maple
p.78 Blaauws juniper
p.81 Stewartia
p.86 Blaauws juniper
Back cover Crab apple

Petra Engelke-Tomlinson:
p.77 Crab apple
p.78 Japanese elm

David Tipler:
p.53 Honeysuckle

Andy Aitken:
p.60 Pyracantha
p.38 Chinese elm

Jim Amos
p.64 Cotoneaster

All other trees are from my own collection.

Some beautiful bonsai pots by Petra Engelke-Tomlinson (Greenwood Gallery) are featured throughout this book.
They are as follows:- p.29 Deshojo maple
p.51 Suiban for San José juniper
p.77 Crab apple
p.78 Japanese elm
p.78 Blaauws juniper
p.81 Stewartia
p.86 Blaauws juniper

To my children Marcus and Carlene. May your journey through the seasons of life be inspiring and fruitful, yet full of wonder.